Homer *for the* Holidays
The Further Adventures of WILSON THE PUG

Wilson the Pug
with Nancy Levine

Skyhorse Publishing

Skyhorse Publishing books may be purchased in bulk at special discounts for sales promotion, corporate gifts, fund-raising, or educational purposes. Special editions can also be created to specifications. For details, contact the Special Sales Department, Skyhorse Publishing, 307 West 36th Street, 11th Floor, New York, NY 10018 or info@skyhorsepublishing.com.

Skyhorse® and Skyhorse Publishing® are registered trademarks of Skyhorse Publishing, Inc.®, a Delaware corporation.

Visit our website at www.skyhorsepublishing.com.

10 9 8 7 6 5 4 3 2 1

Library of Congress Cataloging-in-Publication Data is available on file.

Cover design by Eric Kang
Cover photograph by Nancy Levine

Print ISBN: 978-1-5107-1442-7
Ebook ISBN: 978-1-5107-1446-5

Printed in China

To find out more about puppy mills
and what you can do to help stop them,
please visit www.stoppuppymills.org
for information from
The Humane Society of the United States.

FOR PUG AND DOG RESCUERS EVERYWHERE

Introduction

Hello. My name is Wilson the Pug. Not so long ago, in a land not very far away, I first met my pug puppy pal, Homer. The holiday season was upon us. So while most pugs were happily curled up in a ball, napping in their warm, cozy beds by the fire or enjoying a nibble on gourmet holiday treats, little Homer was lost and alone, wandering the cold streets.

Now as it happened, I was searching for a good deed to do for the holidays—*the right thing*, as it is written in the Tao-te Ching, the ancient Chinese book of wisdom. You see, I am a Taoist pug, from an ancient lineage of Taoist pugs dating back through the centuries to ancient China, around 500 B.C. Back then, my greatest great grandfather, Pug-tzu, was the best friend and constant companion of Lao-tzu, the wise old Chinese philosopher who is usually credited with writing the Tao-te Ching. In fact, it was Grandpa Pug-tzu who inspired Lao-tzu to pen the classic text. Here, then, is how they first came upon this notion of doing *the right thing*:

One day when the great winter freeze was upon the land, Pug-tzu and Lao-tzu set out into their village for their evening walk. They soon came upon a lost puppy, shivering and alone in the road. Pondering what to do, Lao-tzu looked at Pug-tzu, who cocked his head from side to side, as pugs are wont to do. In an instant, the old man realized the answer, saying, "You are so right, my puggled friend. *A virtuous person will do the right thing*," making a mental note to include this insight in his Tao-te Ching, adding, "We must find this puppy a home." And with this, Lao-tzu scooped up the puppy under his heavy wool cloak and set about to find him a home.

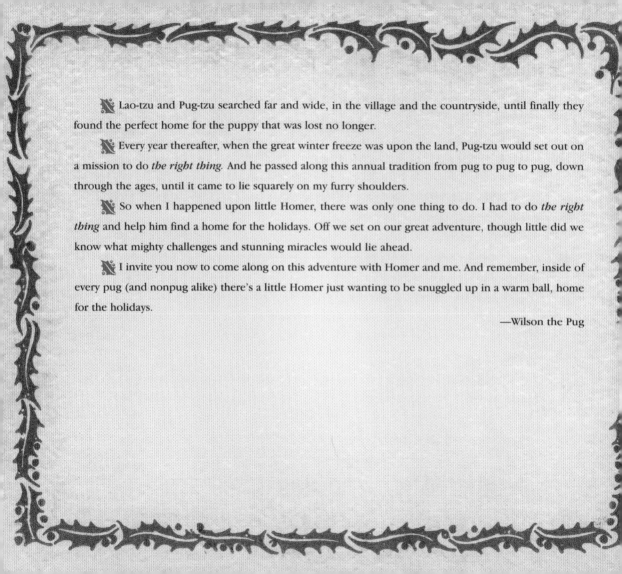

Lao-tzu and Pug-tzu searched far and wide, in the village and the countryside, until finally they found the perfect home for the puppy that was lost no longer.

Every year thereafter, when the great winter freeze was upon the land, Pug-tzu would set out on a mission to do *the right thing*. And he passed along this annual tradition from pug to pug to pug, down through the ages, until it came to lie squarely on my furry shoulders.

So when I happened upon little Homer, there was only one thing to do. I had to do *the right thing* and help him find a home for the holidays. Off we set on our great adventure, though little did we know what mighty challenges and stunning miracles would lie ahead.

I invite you now to come along on this adventure with Homer and me. And remember, inside of every pug (and nonpug alike) there's a little Homer just wanting to be snuggled up in a warm ball, home for the holidays.

—Wilson the Pug

Homer *for the* Holidays

It all began when I was searching, as I do every year, for a good deed to do for the holidays—*the right thing,* as it is written in the Tao-te Ching, the ancient Chinese book of wisdom.

One day, as the winter shadows grew long and gray, I saw something moving around among the Dumpsters behind the bagel store. I couldn't quite tell what it was, but I heard it making little snuffling noises.

As I moved closer, I was able to see more clearly—why, it a was baby pug!

"What are you doing out here all alone, baby pug?" I asked him.

"I don't know. The last thing I remember is escaping out an open gate," he said, lowering his head to sniff a cream cheesy bagel crumb.

"Escaping from what? Escaping from whom?"

"I don't really remember," said the baby pug. "But I think maybe I was trapped in a Gupllim."

"A Gupllim? Well, I don't know what a Gupllim is, but I do know it's holiday time." Then I asked, "Don't you have a home?"

"What's a home?" asked the baby pug.

"A home is . . . ," I tried to explain, "well, a home is like . . . it's where . . ." Then I realized, "A home is like the Tao, baby pug. I can't quite describe it, but you'll know it when you find it. It will just feel right. Oh, and there's lots of cheese there."

"Oh, I see," said the baby pug, his little curly tail wagging just a bit. "Well, then, I would like very much to find this place called home. Cheese is my favorite."

"Well, baby pug, I happen to be looking for *the right thing* to do, so I'd like to help you find a home, too. May I call you Homer?"

"Oh yes, I'd like to be named after a place where there's lots of cheese," said the baby pug.

For a moment I thought about calling him "Wisconsin," but decided Homer was a more suitable name for a pug.

"Come, then, Homer, follow me," I said. "Let's find you a home."

I brought Homer back to my home, thinking this would be a good place to start our search.

"What are we doing?" asked Homer.

"Nothing," I told him.

"Why are we doing nothing, Wilson? I thought we were going to try to find a home for me."

"We are, Homer. But first we must do nothing. The Tao-te Ching says, *'For those who practice not-doing, everything will fall into place.'*"

"Oh, I see," said Homer. "But this not-doing is not so easy for me."

"Someday, when you are a grown-up pug, not-doing will be easy for you, Homer, you'll see."

While we were sitting there, doing nothing, I heard a tiny rustling in a corner of the yard and decided to investigate.

Fred the Turtle was gathering with his family around their Christmas tree. Because the Turtle family is so slow moving, they start coming together in advance of Christmas to make sure everyone arrives on time.

"Fred," I explained, "my friend Homer is looking for a home. Could he perhaps join you and your family for the holidays and beyond?"

"I'm not sure that's such a good idea," said Fred, looking on as Homer sniffed at his eldest son with a bit too much enthusiasm. "Besides," Fred added, "a turtle family probably wouldn't make such a good home for a pug anyhow."

"Perhaps not," I agreed, as Homer reached out a paw, trying to pet Fred's son.

"But I hear Theo the betta fish's bowl is vacant," Fred offered. "Maybe that would make a good home for your friend."

Theo the betta fish had grown up and had a family of his own, so he and his whole family had recently moved into a bigger tank—a co-op, actually, with other fish families. Theo had seemed to thrive in his old bowl, so I thought it might work for Homer.

"You'll know it when you find it. It will just feel right," Homer repeated to himself as he climbed partway into Theo's bowl. Then he turned to me and said, "This doesn't feel so right, Wilson."

"Excellent, Homer. You see, every time you find a home that doesn't feel right, you are one step closer to finding the one that does."

Just then a voice from the neighboring yard said, "Ain't it the truth."

"Come with me, Homer," I said. "There's someone I'd like you to meet."

We squeezed through a loose board in the fence to my friend Henry the Coonhound's yard next door.

"Well," said Homer, as he made himself right at home in Henry's house, "I believe this could be an excellent home."

But Henry was somewhat less certain.

Now, make no mistake, Henry is quite a good sport and a kindly fellow. But when he noticed a fresh small puddle in his house, he said, "I don't know if a coonhound's house is really such a good home for a pug. After all, I'm a pretty big guy, you know. What would happen when I rolled over in bed?"

I nodded in agreement, telling Homer, "You see, when it's the right home, it will feel right to everyone."

We thanked Henry for even considering sharing his house. Homer thanked him in his inimitable puggly way.

We tried all sorts of places in search of the right home for Homer.

I remembered something about an old woman who lived in a shoe. Certainly if an old woman with lots of children could live in footwear, why not a pug?

Homer gave it a try.

"How is it, Homer? Does it feel right?"

"No, I don't think so," he said, his voice muffled by the fleece lining.

"Then why do you keep burrowing in there?" I asked.

He replied, "I have a thing for fleece."

"Well," I told him, "it's not fleece lined, but I know someplace you may find just as cozy."

"This is one of my favorite places, Homer. It's a small but cozy A frame. And if this were your home, you'd be assured of greeting the mailman every single day."

"Hmm, I do love the mailman," said Homer, considering. "But it doesn't feel quite right—something bothers me about being in a small box." Then he said, "I *don't know* how I'll ever find a home."

"Excellent work, Homer. You see, as it is written in the Tao-te Ching, *'Knowing you don't know is wholeness.'* It's all a matter of seeing things through a different lens. Here, let me show you something."

"Look at me, Homer. What do you see?"

"I like your sunglasses, Wilson, but what do they have to do with finding a home?"

"Home is where the heart is," I told Homer. "If you see the world through heart-shaped sunglasses, then wherever you are will always be home."

"I don't really get it," said Homer with a sigh, unable to get the heart-shaped sunglasses to stay on his very small, flat face.

"That's okay, Homer," I said. "I have another dress-for-success idea."

"Congratulations, Homer. You're the homecoming king!"

"Thank you," said Homer, "but what does that mean?"

"Well, if you're homecoming king, it means you're the king of coming home."

Homer thought for a moment, then said, "How can I come home if my home is *no place*?"

"Good point, Homer. But *no place* can be very special. Here, let me show you."

"Now, Homer, I saw this work in the movies once. Do exactly what I do: Close your eyes and click your paws together three times like this and say, 'There's no place like home.'"

"There's no place like home," Homer repeated three times, trying to click his paws together in the ruby slippers. Then he opened his eyes expectantly, but looked down when he realized he was no closer to home than before.

"Sorry, Homer. I guess this trick works only in the movies," I told him. "What we need for you is a real Hollywood ending."

Fortunately, I'd heard about a pug named Roxy, who owned a movie star in Hollywood, Mary Steenburgen.

I thought a Hollywood pug must live a good life, so I contacted Roxy—actually I contacted her assistant, a terrier named Lulu—to ask if Homer might come live with her.

When asked, Roxy said, "Oh, darling, are there really other pugs in the world besides me? Well, I suppose that's fine. But living with one? Well now, that's just silly talk."

Then she said to no one in particular, "I'm ready for my close-up, Mr. DeMille."

Clearly, there was no room in Hollywood for another pug.

"Homer, perhaps yours could be a 'Home, home on the range'? If deer and antelope play there, certainly it must be spacious enough for a pug."

"I don't think so, Wilson. The range may be where buffalo roam, but I don't think it's where pugs sleep," Homer said with a yawn, struggling to keep his eyes open as night crept in.

"Maybe what I really need to feel at home is a bed." Then he asked, "May I share your bed with you, Wilson?"

"Hmm, Homer, have you already tried out this big bed in the bedroom?" I asked.

"Yes, but someone left a newspaper up there, so it wasn't comfortable," he answered.

"Maybe sharing my bed is not such a good idea," I told him. "After all, every pug really should have his very own bed. But you can sleep in my bed for tonight, and in the morning, we'll find you a bed of your very own."

In the morning, we stopped by the Pet Food Express store. "If home is where your bed is, then a whole rack of beds should make an excellent home," I suggested to Homer.

"Yes, these are all very comfortable beds, but a store doesn't feel like a real home," adding, "I want the kind of home where people have to knock first if they want to come in."

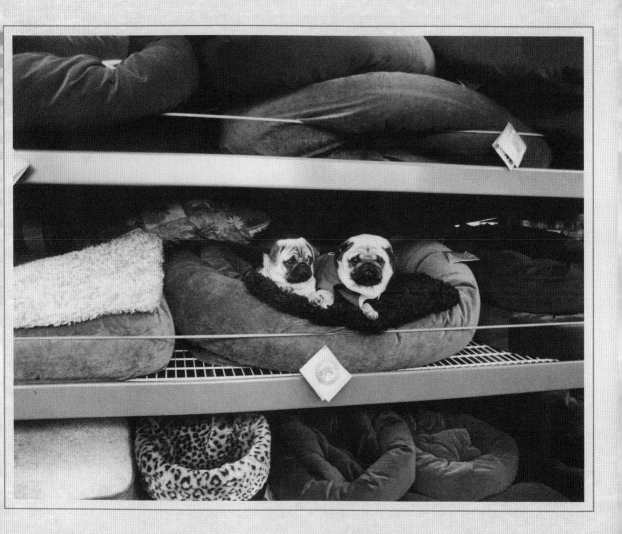

We tried knocking—well, actually scratching—on people's front doors to find Homer a home. "I don't know why no one's answering," I told Homer. "After all, we're not solicitors. We're pugs. I think solicitors have more prominent muzzles."

All the homes we tried were closed up tight. What we needed was a more *open* home.

"Look, Homer, there's a sign for an OPEN HOUSE. Someone must be looking for a pug to come live with them."

Fortunately, I had recently learned to read a little. Homer's reading skills were still a work-in-progress.

"Oh, good," said Homer. "I remember what you said about how the Tao teaches us to watch for signs."

We went inside the open house. There were a few people milling about, opening and closing closet doors. Homer just kept smiling at everyone, hoping one of them was looking for a pug. But to no avail.

Then I heard some people talking. One of them said, "We're preapproved for a home loan."

A home loan, I realized, was an excellent idea. "Perhaps we could simply *borrow* a home for you," I told Homer.

The sign in the bank said HOME LOANS.

We sat patiently and waited for someone to lend Homer a home. But no one did. A few people just smiled and said, "Oh look, aren't they cute."

Finally, Homer started climbing onto the HOME LOANS desk. The security guard didn't find this amusing and escorted us out the front door.

As we were leaving, Homer said, "You know, Wilson, I get bored easily, so a low-interesting home loan probably wouldn't have worked for me anyhow."

"C'mon, Homer, I know a place that's full of excitement and bound to have a home for you."

Surely we could find a home for Homer at the Home Depot. Homer waited outside because no dogs were allowed in. I went into the Home Depot to look at its selection of homes.

The Home Depot seemed to have *everything*. Except a home for Homer. I was, however, delighted to find garden hoses made from recycled tires.

This search for a home for Homer was becoming quite an odyssey.

When I came out of the Home Depot without a home for Homer, he deflated like a pug balloon, his tail uncurling. "Don't worry, Homer. Remember, the Tao-te Ching says, *'The Master acts on what he feels and not what he sees.'* And I have a feeling we should head up into the hills to continue our search."

"I have a feeling that's a good idea," said Homer, with his tail curling back up.

I thought we might have more luck in the woods because many fairy tale endings happen there. So we ventured up the hill into the forest, where soon we were wandering through the snow looking for signs of a home for Homer.

Eventually, we came upon a gnome door carved into a big tree. There were a few tiny gnome Christmas gifts outside the front door, so it looked like a friendly place and perhaps a good home.

We scratched on the door.

"Who goes there?" echoed a gravelly gnome voice from within the tree.

I answered through the door. "Hello, it's Wilson and Homer. We're pugs and looking for a home for Homer."

"A home?" said the gnome. "Ha! I know this trick. I've been chased by pugs on more than one occasion."

Homer's head drooped, and he sat in a pug slouch. Seeing this through the peephole, the gnome opened the door just a crack and told Homer, "Listen, little guy, living with a gnome in a tree is no place for a pug, anyhow. But I'll tell you what. I've got a cousin, an elf, who got a job working with Santa Claus. Come to think of it, you look kind of like an elf. Why don't you give Santa a try?"

And the gnome gave us the address of Santa's satellite workshop, which happened to be just up the road a piece. We thanked the gnome and headed for Santa's place.

When we arrived at Santa's satellite workshop, he agreed to meet with us, even though he was very busy. It was, after all, Christmas Eve, and Santa was doing some last-minute toy making.

"What's on your mind, little friends?" Santa asked. I hopped onto his work-table, telling Homer to wait below; we didn't want any accidents on Santa's table. I explained how we'd been looking for a home for Homer and that I was wanting to do *the right thing* by helping him find one. And I asked if he might have any job openings for Homer.

Santa agreed to give Homer a tryout as an elf. From a cabinet marked ELF WEAR, Santa fetched a size extrasmall elf outfit for Homer and helped him into it.

"Hmm," said Santa, tilting Homer's hat and adjusting his belt buckle. "You look something like an elf, but . . ." Homer flapped his ears back, trying to point them, doing his best elf impersonation. No matter how hard they both tried to make Homer into an elf, Santa just kept saying, "Hmm, almost, but . . ."

Finally Santa paused, looked at Homer, drew on his pipe for a moment and said, "I'll tell you what. Do you have any experience pulling a sleigh?"

Homer cocked his head from side to side as pugs are wont to do.

"Oh good," said Santa, and he opened a cabinet marked REINDEER WEAR.

"Hmm, let's see now," said Santa, fitting Homer with some reindeer antlers. "I'm afraid the wind shear might be a bit much for such a small reindeer."

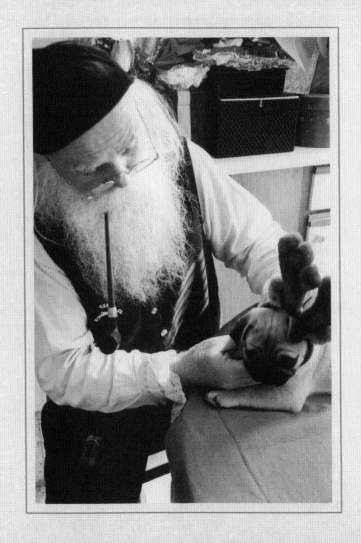

Finally Santa sighed and put Homer down. He motioned for me to hop back up on the table.

"I'm sorry, little fella," Santa told me, "but I can't really hire another elf or reindeer. We've had to cut way back here. But we'll keep his application on file for next year. You might try Roxy the Pug in Hollywood—I heard she may be looking for a new assistant."

I thanked Santa for giving Homer a tryout and headed for the door with Homer by my side. Santa called after us, "You know, the North Pole really isn't such a good home for a pug, anyhow."

Santa had given Homer a souvenir hat to take away with him, but it didn't seem to cheer him up at all. "I don't think I'll ever find a home, Wilson," he said as we headed back down the hill.

"Don't worry, Homer. Things have a mysterious way of always working out for the best. Remember, the Tao is *'hidden but always present.'*"

We wandered back toward town, through the neighborhood of burned-out old factories and barbed-wire fencing. All of a sudden, a black pickup truck screeched to a stop next to us. Two men jumped out of the truck with a huge net.

One of them pointed at us and said, "There he is. Get him," as they swooped in and scooped up Homer into the net.

"Help, Wilson!" Homer cried, "It's the Gupllim! The Gupllim!"

I watched in horror as the men put Homer in the back of the truck and sped away. I ran as fast as I could after them, but the truck soon disappeared around a corner.

I gave chase, but by the time I turned the corner, the truck was nowhere in sight. "How will I ever find my poor little friend Homer? And what is this Gupllim?" I wondered.

I wandered the barren sidewalks, peering down darkened alleys, occasionally calling out, "Homer!" but the only response was my voice echoing through the cold steel factories. I was at a loss for what to do next.

Then I remembered: *For those who practice not-doing, everything will fall into place.* So I sat down, deciding to do nothing for a moment.

And while I was sitting there, doing nothing, a breeze swirled around me. On the crest of the wind, I smelled a familiar scent. Sniff, sniff. "Yes, I recognize it, but what is it?" I thought. Sniff, sniff. I followed my nose up the block and around the corner until I came upon a huge net propped against an old warehouse. There was a big sign posted in front of the warehouse. In red paint it said: PUG PUPPIES 4 SALE. "Could it be?" I wondered. I sniffed and sniffed at the net, realizing all at once—it was the scent of Homer!

Luckily, he had wet the net.

I followed Homer's puppy aroma around the side of the building. I tiptoed on the pads of my paws past the side gate, sneaking behind the warehouse. And there, at last, I saw Homer. He was in a cage with a sign that said YE OLDE PUG PUPPY MILL.

There was an hourglass next to Homer in the cage. This, I figured, couldn't be a very good sign.

I got as close to Homer's cage as I could and whispered, "Don't worry, Homer, we'll get you out of here. Tell me everything you know."

Homer said, "I overheard those two men from the Gupllim talking—"

"Wait, Homer. What is the Gupllim?"

"It says it right here on the sign in front of me—g-u-P and l-l-i-M." Since Homer's reading skills were still a work-in-progress and he had only seen the sign from the inside of the cage, he could only read the words "Pug" and "Mill" backward, as "guP lliM."

Homer continued, "They said they would try to sell me to a last-minute Christmas shopper by tonight, Christmas Eve, for thousands of dollars so they can pay their back taxes. They've already sold all the other dogs and puppies. If they can't sell me by sundown, they will burn this whole place down—with me in it—to collect insurance money!"

Just then we heard one of the pug mill men coming. As I snuck away, I told Homer, "Don't worry, I'll go get help."

"Hurry, Wilson, hurry!" Homer begged.

Out of the corner of one of my rather prominent eyes, I saw the man flip the hourglass in Homer's cage to begin the countdown till sundown.

I ran all the way back up the hill to Santa's workshop to try to get help for Homer.

When I arrived there, Santa was sitting at his bench, reviewing his Christmas Eve to-do list.

I heard him telling one of the elves, "You see, I received a last-minute request from a little girl who's been very, very good this year—she won first place in a kids' cooking contest for her cheese soufflé. Her letter said that since she's been so very, very good, if I'm the real deal, I'll bring her her fondest, lifelong wish for Christmas: a baby pug. But the letter she sent to me at the North Pole got delayed because of drastically increased airport security measures."

The elf shook his head and made a "tsk, tsk" sound.

Then Santa asked him, "How will we ever find a baby pug at this late hour on Christmas Eve? Of course that Homer would have been perfect, but—"

Right then I hopped onto his worktable. "Santa, Homer's in big trouble," I explained. "He's trapped in a pug puppy mill. The people who run the place prey on shoppers' ignorance, overbreeding and mistreating pugs, selling them by whatever means necessary to make as much money as possible to satisfy their greedy appetites!" And I told him about their plan to burn the pug mill to the ground with Homer in it if they didn't sell him by sundown.

Santa said, "Well, I was just now wondering where ol' Homer might be." And he put on his heavy velvet coat and followed me out the door.

Santa and I snuck back behind the pug mill warehouse to Homer's cage. We got there just as the sun was setting and the hourglass was about to run out.

"Can you help him, Santa?" I asked. "Can you get Homer out of here?"

Santa was able to jimmy Homer's cage door.

Just then we heard the pug mill men talking to each other inside. One of them said, "Hey, did you hear something funny out there? Put down that gasoline and go check it out."

"C'mon, Santa, hurry," urged Homer. "Please get me out of here!"

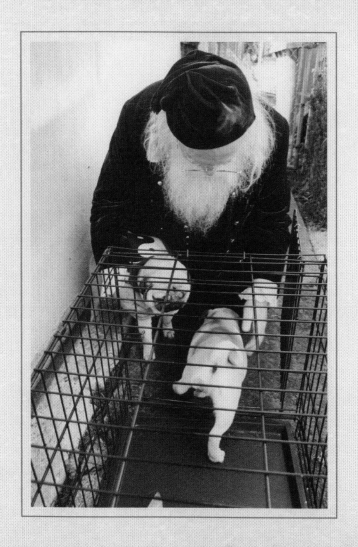

Santa scooped up Homer under his arm and headed out the pug mill gate, checking to make sure the coast was clear. I ran alongside them.

When we were a good ten blocks away, we heard a booming explosion and turned around to see a bright orange fireball shooting up from where Ye Olde Pug Puppy Mill had been.

That night Santa packed Homer and me into his sleigh and we delivered presents to all the boys and girls who had been good that year. I told Santa, "The Tao-te Ching says, *'When people see things as good, evil is created.'*" And we wound up delivering some presents to boys and girls who had not been so good, too.

When we arrived at the house of the little girl who had won the cooking contest for her cheese soufflé, Santa once again scooped up Homer under his arm.

I told Homer, "I have a feeling this may be it, Homer. This may be the right one."

Homer said, "I have that feeling, too, Wilson. If it's right, I'll know it."

"I'll see you in the morning," I shouted after Homer as I watched Santa heading for the girl's chimney with Homer's curly tail sticking out from under his coat. I waited in the sleigh, making small talk with some of the reindeer.

The next morning, the little girl found Homer beneath the Christmas tree among the other presents. She squealed, "Ooo, it's a baby pug! He did it! Santa did it!"

The little girl made Homer feel at home right away. After all, she'd been preparing for years for his arrival. She put a little Christmas collar on him and hoisted him onto the mantelpiece to show him a Christmas stocking with his name on it. (Santa had asked an elf to do some last-minute embroidery.)

"See?" she showed Homer. "You already have your own Christmas stocking." Then she told him, "You look more like a 'Homer.' But I wonder who Wilson is?"

Just then there was a knock at the front door.

Santa had knocked on the door, then hurried toward his sleigh, which was parked behind some bushes. I sat on the front doorstep and thanked him as he headed off. He just chuckled, winked, and waved, then mounted his sleigh and flew off with the reindeer.

When the little girl opened the door, there I was sitting on the welcome mat.

"Oh look! It's another pug!" she squealed. "Come in, come in!"

The girl brought some of her award-winning cheese soufflé out from the kitchen, sharing little bites with Homer and me. After Homer's first nibble, he told me, "Oh, Wilson, this is feeling very right." And he thanked me in his inimitable puggly way.

I thanked Homer for helping me to do *the right thing* for the holidays. Then I bade him adieu, reminding him that we would be seeing each other at pug parties and picnics, of which there were many.

Just before I left, Homer, who was snuggled in the fleecy pajamas of the little girl's lap, said, "You know, Wilson, I think I could get used to this not-doing." Then he added, "This must be home because it just feels so right."

Epilogue

Oh and by the way, the owners of Ye Olde Pug Puppy Mill were sent up the river for tax evasion and insurance fraud. The authorities got a mysterious tip from someone who would identify himself only as "Nick."

Acknowledgments

"The kind person acts from the heart . . ."

TAO-TE CHING, 38

So many wonderful people contributed to the creation of this book. The authors would like to extend their deepest gratitude and appreciation to all of them.

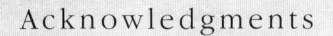 For their kind support, we thank the Home Depot, the Oakland Athletics, the Berkeley Richmond Jewish Community Center, Pet Food Express, Eric Burkhart, Sheira Kahn, FishFirst!, Jeffrey Himmel, Kari Wishingrad and Lenny Cocco, Lisa Sheeran and Frisco Pugs, and our dear neighbors, the Farmer-Messeri Family, and V. Hap Smith.

For their playful participation, we thank the pugs of Marv Albert, Mackenzie Phillips, and Lili Taylor, as well as Suzie Steingruber, the Columbia Tristar Motion Picture Group, and LaMarr Desmond Dekker, the king of all Rottweilers.

Special thanks to our supporting cast, especially Mike Duvall, an extraordinary, multitalented gentleman. We consider ourselves privileged to have worked with him. Of course, thanks, too, to Santa Claus for taking time out from his busy schedule to make an appearance. We're grateful to Suzanne Brady of the Whim Agency for introducing us to both of them. We were honored to work with the profoundly photogenic Roxy the Pug and her staff, Mary Steenburgen and Ted Danson, Rachel Karten, Ira

Liss, Alison Mann, and Melissa Tagliareni. In her debut role, we'd like to thank Isabel Cain, an actress with great promise. Talent must run in the family as her brother, Gabriel Cain, proved an outstanding photographer's assistant. Thanks, too, to their parents, David Cain and Stacie Blair, always, for their support. For his extraordinary patience with pugs, we thank Henry the Coonhound, purveyor of Oh Henry Car Coveralls, and Tamara Romijn.

For their considerable creative and business prowess, we thank our partners at Viking, especially our editor, Alessandra Lusardi, who, with unwavering enthusiasm and encouragement, shepherded this book to fruition. We wish also to thank all of Team Wilson for their vision and dedication, in particular Clare Ferraro, Gretchen Koss, and a trio of very talented designers, Beth Middleworth and Herb Thornby for their jacket artwork, and Jaye Zimet for the book's interior design.

Our sincere appreciation goes to our agent, Arielle Eckstut, who is not only an exemplary adviser and champion but one we feel lucky to call a friend. In kind, we'd like to thank Daniel Greenberg and everyone at the Levine Greenberg Literary Agency for all their hard work.

For their photographic expertise, we thank PhotoLab, Cantoo, and most of all Iris Davis along with Brett Myers of Davis Black and White for their masterful black and white printing.

A special nod of recognition goes to Nancy's first storytelling mentor, the late Spalding Gray, who will be missed but never forgotten.

For daily creative and soul nourishment, we'd like to thank everyone in the Lobby and our circle of friends.

Wilson and Homer would like to thank their families of origin, Jodi Leanne Sorensen and

Treasure Pugs, home of Homer's parents, Peaches and Tomm, and Myrna Powell and School House Pugs, home of Wilson's parents, Heidi and Blaze.

Nancy would like to thank her own family of origin for instilling an inner sense of home from which to draw, her father, the late Irwin Levine, her mother Eileen Levine, and her sister, Fran Herault. Nancy especially thanks Wilson and Homer, who are not only cherished family members but also wise teachers. And in her own favored manner of saving the best for last, we'd like to thank Catherine Woodman, our creative conscience and, for us, the very personification of home.